Pebble®

Great African-Americans

Garrett MORGAN

by Sarah L. Schuette

Content Consultant: Allen Ballard, Professor,
History and Africana Studies, University at Albany

Consulting Editor: Gail Saunders-Smith, PhD

CAPSTONE PRESS

Pebble Books are published by Capstone Press,
1710 Roe Crest Drive, North Mankato, Minnesota 56003
www.capstonepub.com

Copyright © 2015 by Capstone Press, a Capstone imprint. All rights reserved.
No part of this publication may be reproduced in whole or in part, or stored in a retrieval system, or transmitted in any form or by any means, electronic, mechanical, photocopying, recording, or otherwise, without written permission of the publisher.

Library of Congress Cataloging-in-Publication Data
Schuette, Sarah L., 1976–
Garrett Morgan / by Sarah L. Schuette.
pages cm. — (Pebble Books. Great African-Americans)
Includes bibliographical references and index.
Summary: "Simple text and photographs present the life of Garrett Morgan, an African-American inventor and entrepreneur"— Provided by publisher.
ISBN 978-1-4914-0504-8 (library binding) — ISBN 978-1-4914-0510-9 (pbk.) — ISBN 978-1-4914-0516-1 (ebook pdf)
1. Morgan, Garrett A., 1877–1963—Juvenile literature. 2. African American inventors—Biography—Juvenile literature. 3. African American businesspeople—Biography—Juvenile literature. I. Title.
TJ140.M67S38 2015
609.2-dc23
[B] 2014007344

Editorial Credits
Nikki Bruno Clapper, editor; Terri Poburka, designer; Kelly Garvin, media researcher; Laura Manthe, production specialist

Photo Credits
AP Images: AP Photo, 10; Cleveland Press Collections: courtesy of the Michael Schwartz Library Special Collections, Cleveland State University, 12; Cleveland Public Library: Photograph Collection, 20; Getty Images/Archive Photos: cover, 18; Library of Congress: 8; Shutterstock: Marfo, design element; The New York Public Library: The Miriam and Ira D. Wallach Division of Art, Prints and Photographs: Photography Collection, 6; Wikimedia: 4, 14, US Patent and Trademark Office, 16

Note to Parents and Teachers

The Great African-Americans set supports national curriculum standards for social studies related to people, places, and environments. This book describes and illustrates Garrett Morgan. The images support early readers in understanding the text. The repetition of words and phrases helps early readers learn new words. This book also introduces early readers to subject-specific vocabulary words, which are defined in the Glossary section. Early readers may need assistance to read some words and to use the Table of Contents, Glossary, Read More, Internet Sites, Critical Thinking Using the Common Core, and Index sections of the book.

Printed in the United States 5605

Table of Contents

Early Years 5
Grown-Up Garrett 9
Middle Years 13
Later Years 19

Glossary 22
Read More 23
Critical Thinking
Using the Common Core 23
Index 24

1877

born

Early Years

Garrett Morgan was a famous inventor. He was born in Kentucky in 1877. Garrett had 10 brothers and sisters. His parents were freed slaves.

a street in Cleveland, 1901

1877

born

Garrett left school after sixth grade. At age 14 he moved to Ohio in search of a job. Garrett settled in the city of Cleveland. He worked at a sewing machine company.

1877

born

1907

opens repair shop

Grown-Up Garrett

Garrett studied machines all day at work. He invented a new sewing machine and a belt fastener. In 1907 he opened a repair shop for sewing equipment.

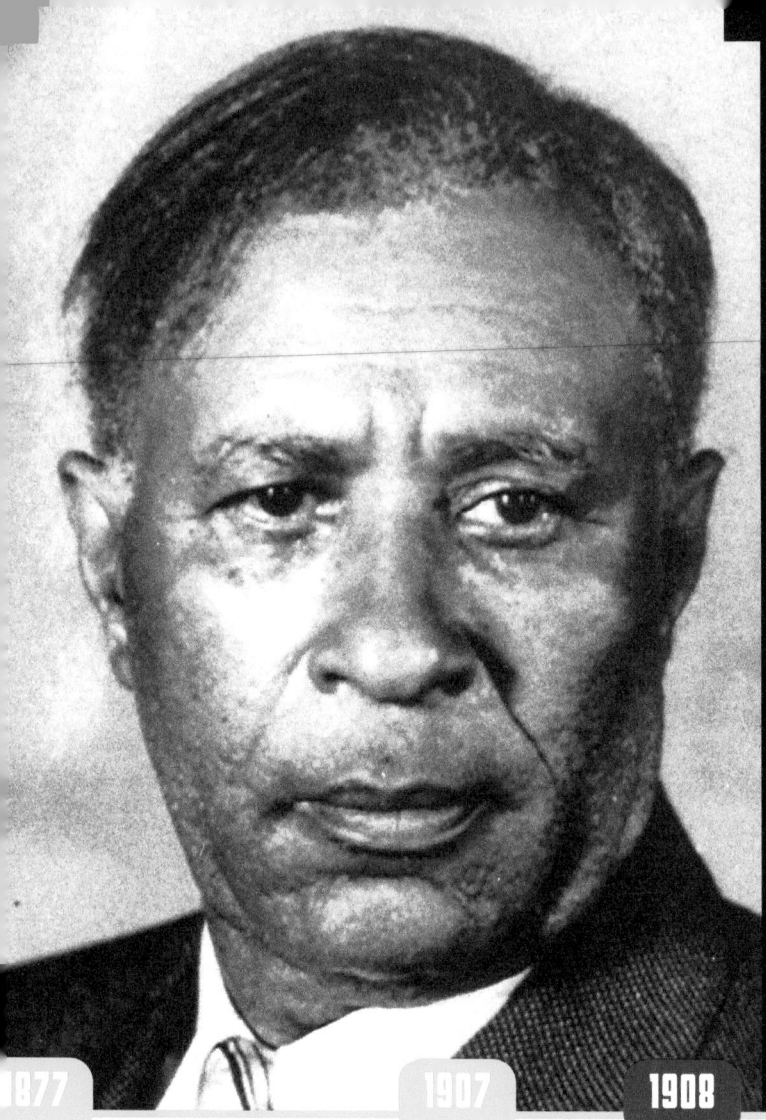

1877

born

1907

opens repair shop

1908

marries Mary Anne Hassek

In 1908 Garrett married
Mary Anne Hassek.
Garrett and Mary Anne
opened a tailor shop.
Garrett also sold a cream
that straightened hair.
He became wealthy.

aring
ood
1907
opens repair
shop
marr
Ann

Middle Years

Garrett's most famous invention was a safety hood. It helped firefighters breathe safely in smoky air. Garrett's safety hood saved many lives. Soldiers used it during World War I.

Garrett rescuing a man from a tunnel

1877
born

1907
opens repair shop

1908
marries Mary Anne Hassek

In 1916 there was an explosion in a tunnel under Lake Erie. Garrett and his brother rushed to the tunnel. They put on safety hoods, went into the tunnel, and saved two men's lives.

saves men
in tunnel

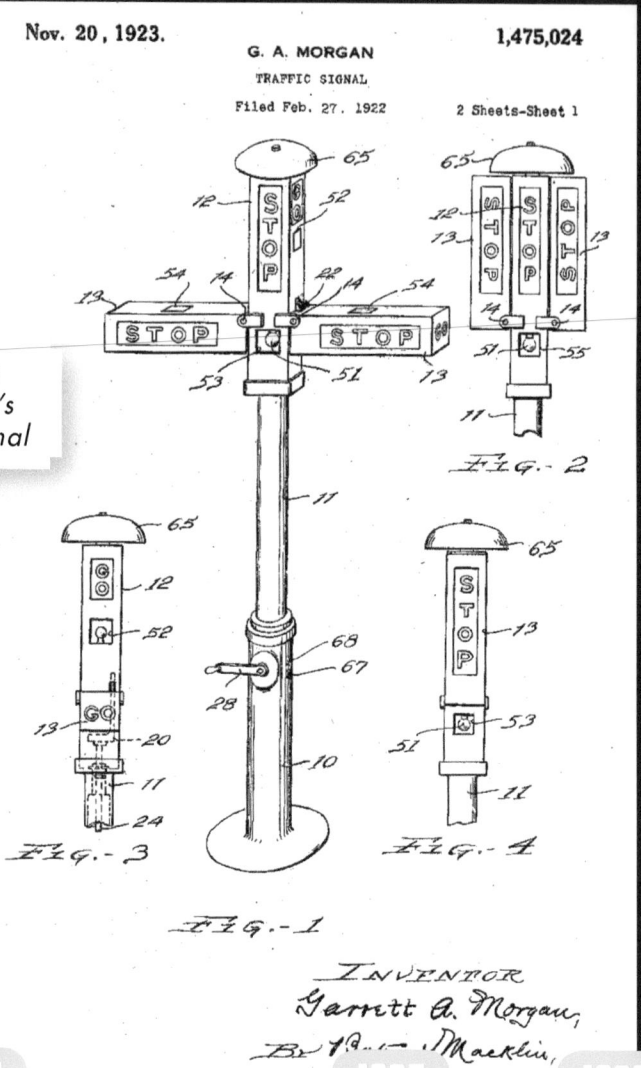

a drawing of Garrett's traffic signal

1877 born

1907 opens repair shop

1908 marries Mary Anne Hassek

In the 1920s there were a lot of car accidents. Garrett wanted the streets to be safer. In 1923 he invented a traffic signal. His signals later became the traffic lights we use today.

1916

saves men in tunnel

1923

invents traffic signal

1877

born

1907

opens repair shop

1908

marries Mary Anne Hassek

Later Years

Garrett was a leader in the African-American community. He started a newspaper called the *Cleveland Call*. He also gave money to African-American colleges.

1916

saves men in tunnel

1923

invents traffic signal

1877

born

1907

opens repair shop

1908

marries Mary Anne Hassek

After a lifetime of inventing, Garrett died in 1963. He is best known for his safety hood and traffic signal. These inventions made the world a safer place.

1916 saves men in tunnel

1923 invents traffic signal

1963 dies

Glossary

community—a group of people who live in the same area

explosion—a moment when something blows apart with a loud bang and great force

fastener—something that attaches two things to each other

invent—to think up and make something new

inventor—a person who thinks up and makes something new

settle—to make a place your home

slave—a person who is owned by another person

tailor—a person who sews clothing

World War I (1914–1918)—the war between the Central Powers (Germany, Austria-Hungary, and Turkey) and the Allied Powers (mainly France, Great Britain, Russia, Italy, Japan, and the United States)

Read More

Abdul-Jabbar, Kareem. *What Color Is My World?: The Lost History of African-American Inventors.* Somerville, Mass.: Candlewick, 2012.

Greenfield, Eloise. *The Great Migration: Journey to the North.* New York: Amistad, 2011.

Ready, Dee. *Firefighters Help.* Pebble Books: Our Community Helpers. North Mankato, Minn.: Capstone Press, 2013.

Critical Thinking Using the Common Core

1. What kinds of businesses did Garrett Morgan start? (Key Ideas and Details)
2. What kinds of information about Garrett Morgan can you find in the chapter called "Early Years"? (Craft and Structure)

Index

belt fastener, 9
birth, 5
business owner, 9, 11
Cleveland Call, 19
community leader, 19
death, 21
family, 5, 15
Hassek, Mary Anne, 11
inventor, 5, 9, 13, 17, 21
jobs, 7
Kentucky, 5
marriage, 11
Ohio, 7
safety hood, 13, 15, 21
school, 7
sewing machine, 9
traffic signal, 17, 21
tunnel rescue, 15
World War I, 13

Word Count: 257
Grade: 1
Early-Intervention Level: 22